I Dig Canals

How women helped save the waterways

Alarum Productions

I Dig Canals

First published May 2020
Reprinted with amendments December 2020

Copyright remains with individual authors, artists & photographers

All rights reserved

No part of this publication may be reproduced, copied, stored in a retrieval system, or transmitted in any form or by any means without prior permission in writing from the copyright holder via admin@alarumtheatre.co.uk

Alarum Theatre
www.alarumtheatre.co.uk

ISBN 978-1-83853-230-7

Book edited by Heather Wastie
Cover design by Laura Ndjoli / Nadia Stone

See also:

Soundcloud recordings
https://soundcloud.com/alarum_theatre

YouTube films
https://www.youtube.com/c/AlarumTheatreUK

CONTENTS

Poem: I Dig Canals by Roger Noons....................................	4
INTRODUCTION..	5
FOREWORD by Carolyn Clark...	6
FOREWORD by Dr Jodie Matthews..	7
Haiku by Jill Tromans..	8
THE EARLY DAYS OF CAMPAIGNING by Kate Saffin..............	9-12
CHILDHOOD MEMORIES...	13-16
CHILDREN...	17-19
ROMANCE	19-20
Poem: "I'll Arrange The Honeymoon" he said… by Elena Thomas...	21
FIRST CONTACT WITH THE CANALS......................................	22
Artwork created by Elena Thomas...	23
Poem: A different way of life by Rajan Naidu..........................	24-25
STOURBRIDGE CANAL...	25-27
BOATS AND BOATING—INCIDENTS AND MOMENTS...........	28-30
WORKING PARTIES...	31-32
Poems: The Waterway Recovery Group, Women's Lib 1972, Ripped Jeans by Heather Wastie....................................	33-36
Poems: Working Party, I Dig Canals II by Roger Noons	37-38
ATTITUDES TO WOMEN...	40
Poem: Rally Queen by Heather Wastie......................................	41
CATERING	42-43
CAMPAIGNING...	44-45
Poems: Waterways not Slaughterways, Lorna Thomas, Felice Pearson by Heather Wastie..	46-48
TAKING ON AUTHORITY..	49
Poem: A Canal Journey with my Mother by Rajan Naidu....	50-52
Poem: Histrionic water by Heather Wastie...............................	53
GLOSSARY/SOURCES/ACKNOWLEDGEMENTS......................	54
ABOUT US..	55
THANKS...	56

I Dig Canals
An acrostic based on snippets of memory from Liz Dodwell

In muddy cold haze

Dudley Canal's tunnel
Inspired a song,
Gotta 'Push Boys Push.'

Couldn't do much work,
Arm broken fending off;
Newly pregnant again
And queasy serving breakfasts.
Looking after babes in carrycots.
Smoke from endless bonfires.

Roger Noons

Dudley Dig & Cruise 1970 Bob May Collection BCN Society

INTRODUCTION

The Black Country has some 100 miles of canals, many of which exist today thanks to dedicated campaigners who wouldn't give up when they fell into disrepair. They formed canal societies, protested, lobbied, dug out weeds, removed tons of rubbish, took risky journeys through tunnels to prove they were navigable... The list of activities is a lengthy one. There are lots of accounts of these campaigners, but until now they have mostly focused on the role played by men.

"I Dig Canals" was a phrase used in the 1970s by waterways enthusiasts. The I Dig Canals project – funded by the National Lottery Heritage Fund – has collected a wealth of stories from and about women in the Black Country and beyond, from the end of the Second World War to the 1970s. Alarum Productions' Co-Directors, Kate Saffin and Heather Wastie, together with Project Manager Nadia Stone, have steered the project, which ran from Autumn 2019 to Spring 2020.

A team of twenty-first century volunteers has helped Alarum record oral histories and memories, summarise and transcribe recordings, and search archives for documentary material. Heather Wastie led the oral history strand, which resulted in twenty full-length interviews with individual women and mother/daughter pairs. Transcribed extracts from those recordings - edited for ease of reading - together with shorter interviews, appear in this book along with documents shared by interviewees and items from the documentary research strand, led by Kate Saffin. The book also includes poems and other creative pieces by Roger Noons, Jill Tromans, Elena Thomas and Rajan Naidu who attended a writing workshop on how to use research material to write new pieces.

The recordings are available in the National Waterways Archive, Ellesmere Port, as a legacy for others to research in the future. Short extracts from the interviews can also be heard in a series of I Dig Canals podcasts on https://soundcloud.com/alarum_theatre

Through Heather's involvement with her family from the 1960s onwards, the company were aware of the important contribution made by women, but the results of this research have exceeded all expectations and Alarum are proud to share a very small percentage of those stories in this celebratory book.

FOREWORD

by Carolyn Clark

These lyrical and evocative accounts bring to life the relatively short moment in history when a small, dedicated band saved a national treasure. Digging with the same tools as the canals were cut out of the earth 300 or more years before was a labour of love for these volunteer navvies.

The stories show it was liberating in deed for women to share the mud and the tea mug, the hollering and hauling, the shovel and the stew... and the love of canals. Everyone had something to give. Getting stuck in with babes in arms, mucking in, 'beavering away quietly in the background', there are proud memories of muck everywhere.

I've shared memories with communities about canals for many years now and this book makes a unique contribution. What these women helped recreate is a glorious Midlands water feature for generations to enjoy. Fifty years on, it's timely the voices of the unsung women are heard. And it's a joy to hear them.

Carolyn Clark is Author of The East End Canal Tales and 'Regent's Canal Heritage' programme manager.

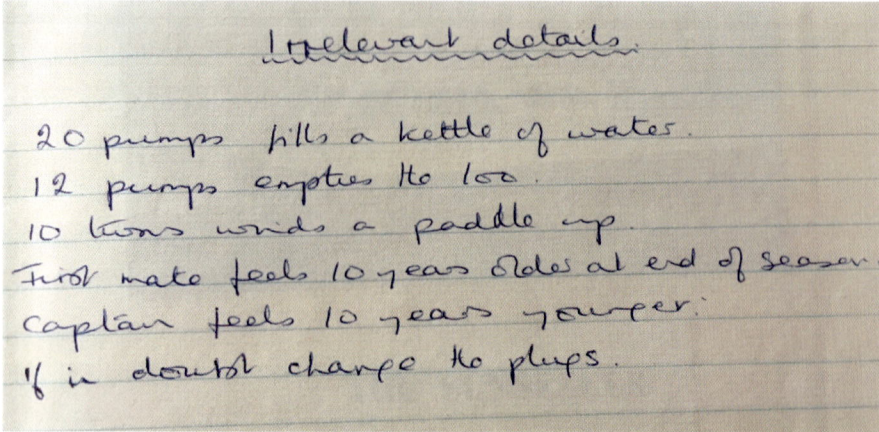

Front page of boat log written by Gillian Whittaker

FOREWORD

by Dr Jodie Matthews

Digging through a familiar landscape, hoping to rejuvenate it, to see it with new eyes and put it to new use: this is, of course, a common strand running through many of the experiences discussed in this book. However, it is also what I Dig Canals has done to the landscape of memory, digging in to female experience in order to see sometimes familiar events through new eyes and recovering the central role played by women in waterways restoration. The stories told here show that the canals are full of feelings and senses: the lovely, dirty joy of sliding down moss into the cut; the smell of a dog after she has swum in the canal; rough work in black mud; the fear of creeping into an unlit chasm; gentle breezes on the skin. The networks described in these valuable testimonies are not just those of connected waterways, but networks of family and friends. There are unexpected treasures in these canal stories: pearlescent shells; tealights in a tunnel; a passing boat horse. There is hard work, solidarity, and care. The restoration got the canals moving; these stories move in other ways, too.

Dr Jodie Matthews is Reader in English Literature at Huddersfield University and Honorary Research Fellow with the Canal & River Trust.

COMMENT January 1967

FOR better or worse, here's number three. You may wonder why some of the pages in this edition have been duplicated and not printed. The answer is of course money, your response so far although good, still falls short of the number required to make the finances of N.N look like breaking even.

For Working Party Group members the February effort is at Stourbridge. I know it's a long way from London, but please make the effort. Although on the outskirts of the Black Country, the flight is most interesting and in some places quite rural. Now is your chance to do some real canal work - To quote the Midlands IWA Journal NAVIGATION "Take part in canal history".

Page 1 of Inland Waterways Association magazine Navvies Notebook No 3, Jan '67. Now renamed Navvies, it will shortly reach its 300th edition.

Quietly dying,
our forgotten valleys,
sliding from our lives.

Magic of water,
trickling through memories,
dampened by neglect.

Jill Tromans

THE EARLY DAYS OF CAMPAIGNING

At the end of the Second World War, after nearly 200 years at the heart of England's industrial landscape, the inland waterways were in decline, with transport moving to rail and road. That decline might have been terminal had it not been for a small band of enthusiasts who, in 1946, formed the Inland Waterways Association (IWA) and began the campaign to save and restore the canals. They were followed by numerous smaller societies and groups who fought for particular stretches of water. The story started with an engineer, Tom Rolt, who converted a working boat, Cressy, into a floating home (much to the surprise of the working boaters who couldn't quite understand why one would have a sitting room, or even more incredibly, a bath, rather than a wage earning cargo!) and set off from Banbury to explore the canals on July 27th 1939. With him was the first woman of our story, Angela Rolt. They had married on July 11th, in secret, because her father was violently opposed, calling her "a whore and strumpet" for wanting to marry a "garage mechanic".

From this trip came the waterways classic *Narrow Boat*. After doing the rounds of publishers in the early years of the war, it languished in a drawer under the bed on Cressy, until he met and became friends with H J Massingham. Massingham was a prolific British writer on ruralism and a poet who introduced him to the publishers, Eyre & Spottiswood, and the book finally appeared in 1944. Rolt was surprised by how well it was received and the amount of fan mail he was sent. The key moment in our story came on July 9th 1945 when Robert Fordyce Aickman wrote to him saying:

Dear Mr Rolt,

My wife and I have just read your book NARROW BOAT with the very greatest measure of admiration and agreement. We are literary agents but seldom encounter a new MS at once so distinctive and so penetrating.

He then goes on to share his own concerns about the state of the waterways and adds that *it has long occurred to me that some body might be founded to promote the welfare of the canals and interest in them.*

He concludes with a lengthy paragraph which boils down to their wish to meet Rolt at the soonest possible opportunity.

Rolt replied with enthusiasm and the two couples met for the first time in August 1945, with the IWA being formed the following February.

Angela and Ray, Aickman's wife, soon formed a close friendship. Many of Angela's letters to Ray are in the Aickman archive as he seems to have kept every scrap of correspondence, but few from Ray survive. They deal with the practicalities of visiting each other including post-war travel and rationing.

> *My dear Ray (please do call me Angela), Thank you so much for your card saying you will bear with us from Nov: 19th-24th. I will bring various foods such as sugar, fats, bacon, eggs and anything else you ask me for...*

And

> *My dear Ray, Thank you so much for your card - I feel guilty about London as there is really no excuse for me to come & it makes work for you - whatever happens don't make up TWO beds for Tom and I. We can quite well sleep in one & have done for the past 6 years!! Think of the pillowcases etc!*

Both women worked incredibly hard, but mostly unnoticed, for the association. Angela set up the first waterways exhibition at the London department store Heal's in 1947 and worked hard on the preparation for the first IWA rally to be held in Market Harborough in August 1950. Ray typed all of Robert's letters until Elizabeth Jane Howard (later a novelist and co-writer with Aickman) was employed in 1948 to work three mornings a week for £2 10s. This was no easy task as Robert would stand over the typist and dictate directly as she typed. *This is far less formidable than it sounds,* Ray later wrote to Barbara Balch, a former school friend in 1953. Her patience with Robert had run out (not least because of his well-known affair with Jane Howard), but, even as she left, she seems to have felt that she should organise care for him so approached Barbara as a possible part time secretary. It *...is much easier than taking letters down in shorthand as the person dictating just waits until you have come to the end of the bit you are typing, instead of dashing on not knowing where you are. Anyone who can type can get this sort of thing going... in a week*. It seems to have worked as Barbara worked for Robert for the next twenty years, another unsung heroine of the canal campaigns.

The IWA grew apace over the next five years with the workload on all involved increasing exponentially. However, Rolt and Aickman had always had differing views on how the campaigns should be approached and cracks began to appear, coming to a head in early 1950 as the association prepared for its first national rally to be held in Market Harborough in August. Angela returned from a visit to Market Harborough on February 7th:

My dear Robert,

I have been away since Monday and arrived back on Wednesday to find Tom in what is known as 'a state'. All I had heard before my departure was that you had offended T very much at the meeting on Friday last when Gould and Lucan were present. What Tom has been writing to you I do not know but it would appear that the fact that I do not always agree with Tom in his differences with you has given him the idea that you are influencing me. You see women are not meant to have minds or any ideas of their own.

Rolt had already written one furious letter to Aickman (followed by another the day after Angela had written) and amidst his accusations that Aickman took everyone for granted he wrote:

I would say without any hesitation that if anyone deserves a medal for what they have done for the IWA it is Ray. No one person in the organisation has done so much as she has and it has been perfectly clear to me for a long time that a great deal of the credit that is accorded to you or to me rightly belongs to her. I certainly appreciate this but I sometimes wonder if you do. This is a conclusion I have reached solely from personal observation.

Aickman replied that *the magnitude of Ray's contribution to the Association (and earlier of Jane's) can be known to no-one better than to me. Such success in life as I have achieved I owe indeed almost entirely to Ray.*

Initially the two women wrote to each other insistent that this feud would not affect their friendship; however, it soon became clear that it could not survive the vitriol these two determined men were hurling at each other. And thus, to a great extent, these two pioneering women from the early days of the IWA and campaigning for the canals have disappeared from history, with only Rolt's second wife, Sonia, who became involved from 1948, remaining in the public consciousness.

Kate Saffin

with thanks to Kit Acott and Lesley Jordan for additional research.

CHILDHOOD MEMORIES

Playing football on the ice

The canal froze over at Dudley Port. The ice was really thick. We played football on there. We weren't scared, it was so solid. It must have been a really harsh winter. There must have been ten, fifteen people on this little patch of ice. We walked that way to school. Rather than walking all the way round, we walked across the canal. You wouldn't dream of it now. There were fish in there and eels, but there were lots of bikes and the water looked dirty. We used to spend a lot of time fishing. I remember once they drained it and my friend Jenny, she'd be about twelve, fell in the mud – thick black mud. We thought, *'Oh no, she's gonna get in real trouble'.* But when she stood up she was completely clean and just her outline was in the silt. She was so relieved because she thought her mom was going to go mad.
Angela Gibson

Sliding down the moss

We used to slide down the moss into the cut. It was lovely, a bit dirty. When I was little, horses used to pull the boats along. You'd still see some in the late 60s. They've filled it in now, the locks and everything.
Anne Bannister & Florence Ralph

Walking the dog

As a child in the early sixties, myself and my father used to walk our Jack Russell dog along the canal. The dog liked to jump in and swim. There was a smell to the canal so we had to give her a bath every time when we got home. I used to go walking with my friends from school, look at Netherton Tunnel and think about going through it. We tried it once, went about a quarter of the way through, didn't like it, turned round and came back because none of us had any torches and it was so dark and scary! Never tried it again.
Carol Daley

In the family

One of my great grandfathers was a boatman. He lived in Tipton but he worked on the boats. There used to be a coal yard here and that was the only time we saw boats and they were dirty – not as pretty as they are now.

June Taylor

The canal at Cookley

In the 1960s my nan and grandad had a caravan at Austcliffe Farm in Cookley on the canal. It was very different to how it is now. It was just two big fields with a few caravans. In the Spring I used to play with the baby lambs in one field. The other field was absolutely full of daffodils. It was gorgeous. My nan and grandad's caravan was right next to a massive oak tree and I lived in that oak tree. If I wasn't swimming in the canal, I was up that tree. It's still there now. It was such a peaceful location. I used to swim and collect mollusc shells – big and flat, mother-of-pearl blue inside – I used to look for a pearl but never found one. I was only about six and I used to walk to Wolverley along the canal on my own. I'd go off for miles, for hours on my own and felt totally safe, was never afraid of the canal. I live on a narrow boat now.

Nichola Hickie

A boat on the driveway

My dad kept a twenty-two foot fibreglass hull on the driveway for many years from the late 1960s. It just appeared one day when I came home from school and I was really excited. I always remember having to take cups of tea out for him. *"While you're here, can you just hold this. Can you hold this steady. Can you get the spirit level for me..."* I learned what various tools were, which was unusual for a girl. He was re-layering the hull all the time because he wanted it to be really, really solid, and, to me, had a fibreglass smell oozing from him for ever more. He built the whole cabin. In the front berth there was a drop down table and all four of us – mom, dad, me and my younger sister - slept in there all together for the first few years. We spent every weekend and every summer holiday that we could on the boat.

Further down the line, he took the outboard engine off and installed an inboard engine using one from a Ford Anglia car. He bought the car specifically, ran it for a little while first. I remember tinkering about and helping him with that.

Sue Blake

Swimming

Some girls went swimming in the canal but we'd never say that we did because we'd have got cremated! You'd have your money for going to the baths but you might be tempted to go in the canal and have a swim. The locks that used to be there were just above the swimming baths so we'd go swimming in the lock rather than pay fourpence to go to the baths. We'd probably go and buy some cakes with the money.

Mavis Phillips

Foam

When we had the cruiser in the 1960s we had to be careful in locks not to wind the paddles up too quickly. If we churned the water up too much, lots of foam would be created because of all the chemicals in the water. I remember one occasion when the boat was completely covered in foam! And it left behind dirty marks too.

Heather Wastie

Jocelyn (steering Vesta), Suzie, Ian, Jane & Anne Sinclair.

Life at Ashwood Marina

In the late '60s, early '70s the majority of used boats that were sold by my father were cruisers. As part of the handover process, my father would always do a trial run with the new owners which would mean going from Ashwood through Rocky Lock – where dad would show them how to use a lock – and down to Gothersley Lock. We would then disembark off the boat, he would see that they got through the lock safely and they would go off for their inaugural cruise. I always went along and had a joy ride, sitting on the front of the cruiser, dangling my feet over the edge of the boat and holding on to the pulpit rail. That was a treat that I was allowed most weekends. Mum would always come and pick us up.

If your parents had a boat, you had a dinghy and we'd all potter up and down in them. Some smart kid had an outboard on theirs, so we tied all the dinghies together and there were about ten dinghies going up and down!

Sammy Rose who now runs the business

Suzie, Ian, Jane & Anne Sinclair standing on ice alongside their family boat, Vesta, at Ashwood Marina, Winter 1962.

Entry by Penny Clover in the boat log (usually written by her dad) when she was working towards her Silver Sword (IWA award) as a teenager in 1968.

CHILDREN

The pink coat

When they were working on the Stourbridge Canal, we were there digging, and Rachel was in her pram. She was one. I remember one day she'd got a pink coat on – ridiculous really. As people were walking past they were talking to her and tickling her under her chin. And when I got her back home she looked as if she had been digging the canal. The only clean bit was her feet.
Ann Edwards

Tea lights and a plastic mac

We decided to go on the protest cruise into Dudley Tunnel. It was an open boat and I'd got two children – David was three

and Heather was seven. The towpath was dreadful and we had to climb over a broken bridge to get to the tunnel. So I wondered *'What on earth am I doing here!'* We got on the boat, and somebody had been through the tunnel first, putting little tealights all along the ledges. It was really lovely. David wasn't tall enough to see over the gunwales (the ledge all the way round the boat for you to walk on) so he kept wanting to be picked up. I was wearing a white plastic mac and as I picked David up, put David down, picked him up, put him down, his shoes went up and down my mac. There was red oxide in the bottom of the boat – all wet, like mud – so when we came out the other end I was red all the way down the front of my mac!
Sheila Smith

Children's birthdays – log extract

29th July: Ian's birthday. Arrived Mount Sorrel 12.30 in bad tempers. Inspected damage to the propeller shaft. Two bolts sheered. Went shopping in a hurry as it was early closing. Ian had a wash down with a hose as he had been playing in the coal. Off again at last 3.30pm the boat falling to pieces.

14th Nov: Les Allen cut wire off propellor with oxyacetylene torch. Off about 9.30. Jane's birthday. Steady progress until the pound above the Bratch, which was virtually empty, but we managed to struggle through. Arrived Ashwood in bright moonlight about 7.00pm
Jocelyn Sinclair

The Bolinder and Lucy

It takes quite a hefty kick to get a Bolinder going. My daughter Lucy, when she was older, used to do it. And you've got to know your engine, you've got to listen to your engine, you've got to catch it at exactly the right time to keep it going. They're basic. They were built so that the boatmen could repair them if anything fairly minor went wrong. But the trouble is, they vibrate so much that if you put a cup of tea on the cabin roof it hops and hops and hops and goes over the edge. When Lucy was a baby, she'd sleep through the sound of the engine – if you switched it off, she woke up.
Mavis Waldron

Tina Gittings

Breastfeeding at TRAD

It was Easter '73: TRAD – the Tunnel Reopening At Dudley – the big celebration. I was there selling tickets on my own, with my four-month-old baby who was breastfed. There were hundreds of people coming at me, desperate to get a ticket to go into Dudley Tunnel, and this little bundle of noise going red-faced in the background.
Tina Gittings

ROMANCE

Draining Gear Oil

When I first started boating in 1977 we would have to pole the rubbish out of the way to get through some of the Birmingham loops. The main line was always okay. When we had outboard motors, I lost count of the number of shear pins which got broken because we got something round the prop. If you managed to go a couple of miles without breaking a shear pin you were doing well. The first time I went out with Graham on his boat, it was March, it was snowing, and the shear pin went. I had to use my tights to strain the oil to get all the bits of swarf out because he'd forgotten to bring any more oil with him. So my first introduction to boating was freezing cold, snowing, on the towpath in Edgbaston draining gear oil through my tights.
Jeni Hatton

A dinghy in Dudley Tunnel

1963/64 I left school and started going out with this lad who was involved with exploring Dudley Tunnel at the time. He had a canoe which he would take to the tunnel on a Sunday. The very first time I went there, I was in what was supposed to be a one-man rubber dinghy – it was more like a floating doughnut. I sat in that with a tow rope back to the canoe and off we went; it was only a one-man canoe, you see. You can never appreciate the splendour of Cathedral Arch in Dudley Tunnel until you have seen it from water level. When I say water level, my bum was actually below water level in the cold water.

That relationship went through a dodgy patch. Basically, one time, he went into the flooded mine so he could explore it, while I stood on a dry patch and waited. After a long time he hadn't come back and I could see it was getting dark outside so I headed out and as far as I know he might still be there. (I have seen him since. I do know he's out really.)

First date

My new boyfriend Derek, his brother and their mates had borrowed an old wooden boat, Beatrice, from Gas Street Basin intending to tow it all the way to Stourbridge because they wanted to prove the right of navigation. They hadn't got a boat of their own. They had made it through some of the locks successfully, but got into one lock, which had moved due to subsidence, and the Beatrice was a bit too wide so it got absolutely stuck. No way in, no way out. Len Wall, the Waterways Manager at the time, wrote to Derek's brother saying, *Your boat is obstructing the right of navigation. Please remove it.* So I got taken on the bus to Stourbridge which, living in Tividale, was a very foreign land and, basically, we had to drain the lock, chop the Beatrice up, bring the wood out and burn it. That was my very first date with my husband. It was years later before we realised that Len Wall was actually on our side and this was his way of giving us the right of navigation.

Tina Gittings

"I'll Arrange The Honeymoon" he said...

It certainly wasn't the right gear
For finding the boat without lighting
Then I couldn't find the bed
(I'd brought my super-scanty nightie)

I needed a strong arm to make it up
But I didn't have one handy
I was no use either at the lock
He yelled "I wish you were a man, dear!"

I did survive the fortnight
I found that I enjoyed it and
The bugs around the narrow boats
Had me well and truly bitten

Now conversations over dinner
Are of the one track kind
Of London Navvies, working parties
And second place is mine

Elena Thomas

Words found in an article by Jane Godwin
Waterways World October 1972

FIRST CONTACT WITH THE CANALS

Shear pins

It was an outboard engine and if you hit anything in the water and it was going to stop the engine, it used to break a little pin called a shear pin. To get out of the basin onto the main Staffordshire and Worcestershire Canal, it was very very weedy. So we'd set off for an afternoon cruise and after about five minutes we'd break a shear pin. So we'd have to change it, have another go, and five minutes or so later we broke another shear pin, so we didn't get out onto the main line for a long time and we kept running out of shear pins!

Sheila Smith

Sheila Smith and family with their first boat, early 1960s at Autherley Junction, known as 'Cut End'

Created by Elena Thomas in response to short extract from our interview with Jeni Hatton

A different way of life
Words found in our interviews with Sheila Smith

Get away on the boat

In the countryside
You can't go fast
You can't go fast
Even if you want to
Nice and slow
Away from The Rat Race
Away from The Telephone
Getting away from it all

Often
A boat would get stuck
Under a bridge
And all the rest
Stuck behind
It was a real battle
On another
Very, very wet weekend

We bumped into some boats
All moored up
Some lady came down the towpath
To greet us
Staffs and Worcester Canal Society
Would you like to join?

A bit further down the canal
Another lady
You can't moor here!
Very officious she was
She said
You can't moor here!

We don't want to moor here
We just want to change the shear pin

I DON'T CARE IF YOU'RE SINKING
YOU CAN'T MOOR HERE!

She was from the Yacht Club
All Big Boats there

Rajan Naidu

STOURBRIDGE CANAL

My real association with the canal came when Graham and I got married in 1966 and we came to live with our garden going down to the Stourbridge Canal which at that time was derelict and basically mud and rushes. I can't think that there was that much debris in it because there was so much mud. Graham started to clear it because it had what we call doodlebugs – great big mosquitos – and he had a very nasty bite which he was allergic to, so we'd got to get rid of this stagnant water. So he started to dig.

Stourbridge Stop

Over many months of Staffs and Worcs Canal Society committee meetings, we produced a campaign document called the Stourbridge Stop and I wrote the script. When it was printed, we had a group of Society members down here, colouring in the maps. I ran the Society shop for many years and organised the Society stand – three display panels with pictures, maps and relevant information – which I took round to various events, not necessarily canal events. You had to send away to get photographs printed in those days which was quite expensive, especially to get enlargements, which we did at our own cost. It was a matter of spreading the word and getting people who took the canals for granted to see that they weren't just 'stinking ditches' and could be an asset.

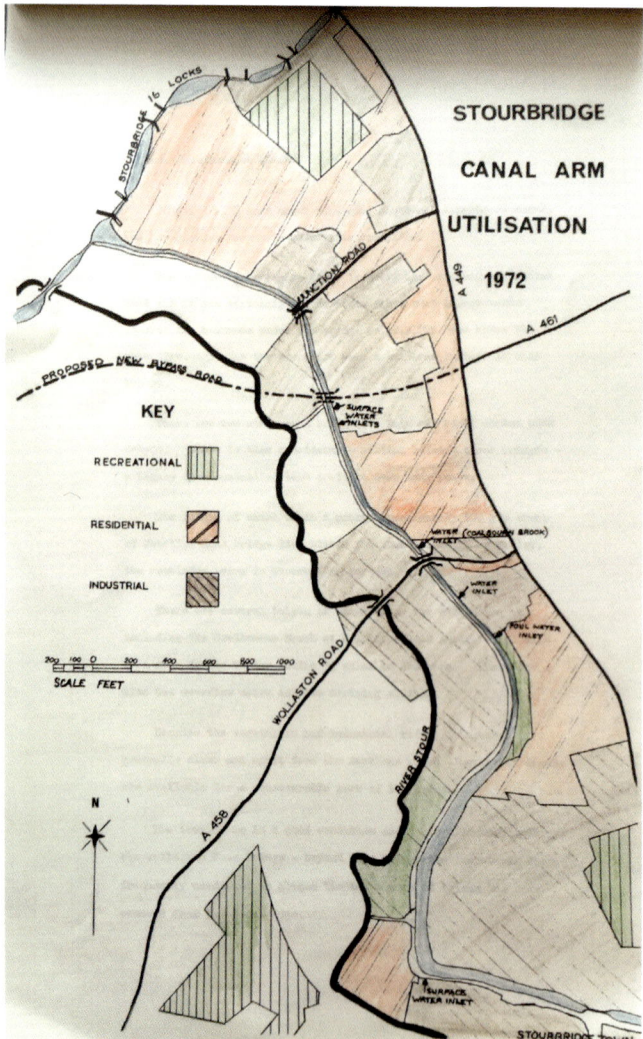

Extract from Stourbridge Stop, hand coloured during meetings at Jose Wyles' home

Housing and feeding the work party

We pushed all the furniture back in the living room and bedroom, and they were all in sleeping bags. It was like '*Ten in the bed and the little one said...*'. Graham cooked a proper fried breakfast for everybody before they went off to work. In those days we had a solid fuel cooker and when they got cold they came up and had a warm in our kitchen.

It was a trek to get by land to the canal so we provided refreshments on the canal towpath. We had tubs from a wholesalers that were instant soups – oxtail, chicken, mushroom... and I got big flasks of boiling water to make the soup. And of course, what do waterways workers want? Bread pudding! We had mountains of bread pudding which I made. So we fed the army.   **Jose Wyles**

Stourbridge Rally 1962

For years after, people mentioned Stourbridge rally and they all replied MUD! It rained a lot and my father Stan Clover was on the IWA Midlands Branch and on the rally committee, organising the trade tent.

I remember going through the Stourbridge 16 locks which were derelict and almost unusable. We had to put tarpaulins over the gates, they leaked so much. One gate had a balance beam that had been set on fire and half burnt. (The suspect was British Waterways but not proven.) I think the Rally Harbourmaster was George Andrews of Wolverhampton Boat Club and his wife Olive organised some trips around the area by coach for boaters attending the rally. I especially remember going on a visit to a local crystal glassworks. As the little girl (aged seven) on the trip, I was given a swan made for me by one of the craftsmen. I have had it on my dressing table ever since. The rally was my first time running around, looking at boats and selling raffle tickets to the public to raise funds for the campaigns.   **Penny Clover**

The swan today, by Penny Clover

BOATS AND BOATING—INCIDENTS AND MOMENTS

Log book extract – Launching Poppin

Launched on Saturday 2nd May at 3pm by Sheila Smith at Brettell Lane, Brierley Hill. It was beautiful weather – the first Spring day of the year.

Maureen Griffiths with Sheila's son, David and son Mark in the hull of narrow boat Laurel

15th May. Poppin was 'eased' under the bridge onto the main canal. It took half an hour to actually get her through. Six months hard work almost ruined! Roger was trying out a borrowed engine and ran the bows into the bridge putting a hole the size of his fist just on the water line. A patch was put on and appears to be satisfactory. This will have to be fibreglassed at a later date.

16th May. We made a start about 10.30 on our way to the Annual Rally of the Staffs and Worcs Canal Society. Approx 100 yards later the engine had to be stopped as it was overheating. We then hitched up to Laurel [the Smiths' restored working boat] and continued on our way. We only got stuck once before the Stourbridge 16 locks and were helped by two young men in a Dawncraft boat. These men towed Poppin down the 16 and we locked through with them. They left us at the bottom of the 16 and that is when our trouble started. Roger managed to get the engine going again and Laurel set off ahead. There was very little water in the pound and every few yards she got stuck. Sheila, Heather and myself rocked Laurel most of the way to the four Stourton locks and Roger was nowhere in sight. I walked back and found he was bow hauling Poppin and had done so since the beginning of the pound. There was something else wrong with the engine.

Maureen Griffiths

Taking the blame

I was sitting in the loo and suddenly a branch of a tree came through the window and I heard my husband's irate voice saying, "*That's your fault!*" And I said. "*Why?*" He said, "*You haven't pushed off the boat.*" I said, "*Well you didn't tell me we were even starting!*"

Pioneering

The waterways were very clogged; people used them as rubbish tips. Pioneers like Tom Rolt, and canal societies like the Staffs & Worcs started to improve them. We were pioneers in those days and there were all sorts of things the canal societies did, like an IWA scheme to encourage you to go further up derelict canals and earn a Silver Sword. That was one of my husband's ambitions. Sitting on the front of the boat on a cold winter night with a broom to break the ice was not quite my idea of fun but at least we did get a Silver Sword going to Cannock Chase.

Gillian Whittaker

Getting stuck

I can remember going along one of the Birmingham canals in the cruiser and the boat went straight over the top of one of those big cable drums. It was going round and round like the London Palladium. The only way we could get it off was for my sister and I to get off the boat and pull with the rope, rocking the boat from side to side.

I will always remember going to dig the Dudley Canal. I was twelve at the time and I was driving a dumper truck. I was in heaven. We dug mud and stuff out of the canal and it was such fun. After that, dad bought me a grappling hook for my birthday.

Caroline Whittaker

Falling in

I fell in at Oldbury. Glyn was working at Les Allen's yard, fitting cabins on the boats. Because I was teacher training, I had lots of holidays and used to go down to the yard, stand and watch or pass a tool etc. I'm hopeless when there are accidents, and

John, Les Allen's son, fell whilst working on a boat. Everyone gravitated to him to see if he was all right and I was left standing on the side of the boat that Glyn was working on. Imagining the worst, I fainted and fell in the canal. John wasn't badly hurt. Glyn came back and could just see my jumper in the canal and had to go in and fetch me out because the water hadn't brought me round.

It was very cold – January or February – I'd got fur hat, coat, boots and everything. At that time, it was the phosphorous run through Oldbury and the water was probably quite warm. I had to go into the shed that the men used and strip off completely. I borrowed some sandals from Les Allen's son Bob, somebody's bib and brace and somebody's jacket because I'd got nothing with me to change into, and I was taken home.

Rosemary Phillips

Engine trouble

We took Roy's mother out for a day trip and couldn't understand why every few yards the engine would pack up. It was a new outboard engine. Then I suddenly realised that every time it had stopped, his mother stood up and it started again, and we realised that she was sitting on the fuel pipe.

Jean Dobbs

Leaking locks

When I started boating, the only time you closed gates was if the lock was leaking badly. On one occasion we were going up, I think it was a trip up towards Titford, and we were going through a lock somewhere or other and it was leaking like a sieve. We used to carry a big sheet of plastic with a couple of strings tied to the top corners and push it down on the upstream side – if it was a top gate leaking – push it down in the water and let the pressure of the water hold it against the gate, then put the paddles up and then the water would hold it there and you could fill the lock. It wasn't quick but it was better than having it pouring in through a hole in the gate. Obviously if it was a bottom gate you'd drop on the inside of the lock – same sort of thing. There were things like that that you just did because it got you by, and you managed to get round the system like it.

Beryl McDowall

WORKING PARTIES

Sickles, scythes and mayors

I set out to dig – on the big Dudley Dig at Parkhead. It was just me on my own and I'd got a Mini. I parked up and said, "*What do you want me to do?*" And they said, "*We've got some scythes and sickles and we want the vegetation cut down.*" So I picked up a sickle and you'd have had a job to cut soft butter with it. So I said, "*Have you got a stone to sharpen it with?*" "*Oh yes,*" they said and produced a stone, and I sharpened the sickle. I'd just got it to a stage where it was really nice and somebody came up and said, "*Oooh, a sharp sickle,*" picked it up, walked off and left their really blunt one, which was even worse than the one I'd done. So I started on that and got it really nice, and someone came up and said, "*Oh you're the woman who sharpens the sickles!*" I didn't dig a single thing, I didn't cut a single blade of grass, but I didn't half sharpen some sickles and scythes!

Along comes the official party to put their blessing on the project and it consisted of a string of mayors. They had come along by boat to the site. When they had shaken lots of hands, said wonderful words etc, somebody said, "*Has anyone got a car?*" I said "*Yes. Why?*" They said, "*Could you take one of the mayors back to his official car?*" I said, "*Look, it's a Mini.*" They said, "*He's not worried – he just wants to get back to his official car.*" So I said, "*Okay. You're welcome.*" This mayor – quite a nice chap – said, "*You don't mind if I bring a friend, do you?*" Another mayor. I said, "*I'm quite prepared to take you but it is a Mini.*" He said, "*It doesn't matter.*" I was just about to set off when another two appeared, so I ended up with four mayors – none of them small – in my Mini. I put the biggest one in the front with me and the other three squashed in the back somehow. The joy of the situation was arriving at the point where all the official cars were, with the official chauffeurs, and the look of sheer amazement on their faces.

Margaret Clark

A happy time

My friend Jackie was a very elegant girl, always beautifully turned out. I've got a photo of Jackie in her nice clothes absolutely plastered in mud, and a great big smile. We were all happy. It was a happy time.
Jose Wyles

Improvised beds

We did a working party on the Stourbridge. My mother thought I was terrible *"taking a child to a thing like that"*. She had a whale of a time. We were supposed to go for the night in a territorial army building but there had been IRA damage so we all had to go round the town in different places. We were in the gas showrooms and it was great because the heating had been left on – it was March. I had taken a sleeping bag but nothing to lie on so we went round the factory and found lots of corrugated brown paper and made up a bed. The chap next to me had brought his silk pyjamas and changed into them every night! It was a wonderful weekend.
Mavis Waldron

Droitwich Dig 1973 by Rosemary Carden

The Waterway Recovery Group

I have personally barrowed concrete,
repointed bricks in a culvert,
balanced on a plank,

manned a bucket-hoist full of unspeakable
ooze from the bottom
of a lock

Young and broke in the 1970s,
many a strenuous weekend was spent
with passionate, beery volunteers

whose devotion restored
stretches of canal which haughty government
had ignored.

In that recessionary, heritage-blind
decade, the group's devotion
can be measured by the fact

they bought their JCB digger
with several million
Green Shield Stamps.

When sunshine package holidays were the trend,
crawling along a narrow ditch in iffy weather
was understood as a pleasure

by relatively few.
But they were right, the anoraks,
we've got them to thank

for this peace.

Heather Wastie

Words found in articles by Libby Purves in The Times:
Unlocking our canals, Tuesday, January 21, 1997
We've got the navvies to thank for this peace, Thursday, July 24, 2008

Right: *Ashton Attack (ASHTAC for short) saw approximately 1000 people work on the Ashton Canal and the Lower Peak Forest Canal over a single weekend in March 1972, by Harry Arnold.*

Below: *The Droitwich Dig 1973, by Rosemary Carden*

Women's Lib 1972

No skirts to be seen
on this cold, grey morning
but these dirty women
are no shrinking violets

beneath the mud
it's hard to tell
men from girls
girls from men

young or old
slim or stout
plain or pretty
in functional clothing

jeans and sweaters
oilskins, anoraks,
bobble hats, macs,
colourful caps

protecting their hair
from flying mud
no fashionable choice
for canal-clearing clobber

the girls still manage
to look attractive
where Women's Lib
comes into its own

joining queues
of ravenous navvies
clamouring for nosh
in Henry's café

or waiting to soak
in Municipal Baths
and suitably cleansed
to raise a glass.

There is no doubt
these girls believe
their contribution
is valuable

as they settle down
in makeshift beds
in the old gas showroom
an unlikely place

for blossoming romance
attracted by the chance
of making new friends
of the opposite sex

all are determined
to make their mark
on the Ashton Canal
which makes many a mark

on them

Heather Wastie

Words found in 'Woman's World at ASHTAC' by Jane Godwin, Waterways World Spring 1972

Ripped Jeans

No gloves
No hard hat
Let loose with a load of scythes

Swinging them
With no instruction
When suddenly

A whack on my bum
Sends my wallet
Flying from my back pocket

Turning round
There's Jane
Looking guilty

Without that sturdy leather
I'd be in casualty
And the rip in my jeans would be

Memorialised
In more than just
A photograph

Heather Wastie

Words found in our interview with Hazel Platzer

Droitwich Dig 1973 by Rosemary Carden

Working Party

unfeminine work;
scruffy, stiff, exhausted.

cutting down trees,
stoking fires
burning branches
digging mud out of locks
pushing dodgy wheelbarrows
controlling crane contraption

in exhilarating surroundings;
healthy work.

Roger Noons

*Words found in A Bird's Eye View by Liz Dodwell
(Navvies magazine, Nov 1966)*

A BIRD'S EYE VIEW

I wonder if other wives, girl-friends or mothers grudgingly pack lunches when a working party comes round, but come home exhausted and very satisfied with the day's effort. It certainly seems strange to enjoy a day cutting down and burning trees or digging mud out of locks, but all the women that go certainly seem to. It's true that one becomes utterly unfeminine, gets filthy, and is so exhausted and stiff that it's a wonder supper gets cooked that evening; but what's that to the satisfaction of a healthy day's work in the exhilarating surroundings of a canal towpath.

The main point is there's plenty a woman can do at a working party. No one will ever stop you cutting down trees, but anyway there are fires to be stoked and many other jobs we can do. I certainly appreciated the hour I spent working the crane contraption they use on the locks at Stourbridge, and even if those wheelbarrows did some dodgy things, it wasn't me who tipped the contents of one on to the enthusiast below.

That of course brings me to another thing- scruffy they may be, but there's nothing wrong with the company. A handy Pub at lunch-time or in the evening on a weekend jaunt, and what more could anyone ask from a weekend out? So if your menfolk contemplate coming on a working party, encourage them, and above all come too.

Liz Dodwell.

I Dig Canals II
Words found in our interview with Jane Henderson

Beginnings

first canal encounter
picking out old prams and bicycles
with Hazel and Rosemary

twelve years old
wearing flares and wellies
getting muddy and tired

on the Grand Union Canal
being away from home
we loved getting dirty

schoolgirls
doing something adventurous
spending weekends together

The Droitwich Dig

loads of people
camped in army barracks
sleeping bags on the floor

working near a lock
no protective clothing
not even hard hats or gloves

pretty rough work
in black mud
exciting but smelly

big canteen for nosh
basic canal rations
can't remember details

I went home
watched Nationwide on telly
and there I was

surprised my parents
they were astonished
at my enjoyment

Spreading the Word

at school I spread the word
wanting to create awareness
importance of restoring canals

one teacher was keen, but
wanting to talk about it
school friends thought I was mad

Conclusion

following years
there were digs, but often
couldn't get to the sites

one summer holiday
spent on the Stratford Canal
sleeping bags in village halls

driving piles, shovelling sand
mixing concrete, pointing bricks
I can still do that

when I left school
I wanted different holidays,
but no regrets

I love the countryside,
not afraid of hard work,
still walk along the towpath

Roger Noons

Mavis Waldron (pictured) on the Stourbridge 'arm'

The water tank was abandoned, so it was dragged up and put in the canal as a workboat. She's holding this rope as there was no engine or anything. That's the only way she could get along.

Jose Wyles

RAFFLE PRIZES

As usual at this time of the year, Rosemary Philips is desperately short of raffle prizes. So please sort out those unwanted oddments (spare husbands are a particular favourite with the lady members) and give them to Rosemary at the October Meeting.

16.

Extract from Staffordshire & Worcestershire Canal Society magazine, Broadsheet, October 1975

ATTITUDES TO WOMEN

In Dudley Tunnel with the band

A group was formed with Glyn, Pete Dodds – another member of the Dudley Canal Tunnel Preservation Society – and Tony Gregory. They were called Gasworks Revival. They liked to sing folk songs going through the tunnel and together they made up the tunnel song Push Boys Push which is now quite famous. Their only paid gig was a booking by the Round Table. They all got on the boat at the Dudley end and part way through the tunnel the band started singing, but the men were just chatting amongst themselves; they didn't seem to be really interested in the songs which was quite disappointing. On the way out I heard someone say that they thought I was the stripper and when was the stripper coming on? I was the only girl that had gone in with them. It's not something I would ever do. I don't know what had given them the idea that there might be a stripper on board because they only paid for a group. I don't know what Glyn thought of it either. We were married then.

Rosemary Phillips

The Waterway Recovery Group now

One of the things about the Waterway Recovery Group which I really like is that, even though I'm a woman in my older years, they see that as a normal thing and don't stop me doing anything. I've never heard anyone say, "*Oh you're a woman you can't do this*" – that equality is unwritten and unsaid. Because you're a woman you don't have to be the cook or do the washing up or clean the accommodation. We sleep male and female together and I've never had any worries apart from the snoring, and we all snore!

Sue Blake

Rally Queen

Not the best attire for boating -
tight short skirt
tiara and stockings
high heeled shoes
precariously posed and pretty

Rally Queen
centre of attention
figurehead on a cruiser cabin
best of three
smiling, waving, later she

will give out prizes for
cruiser handling,
best galley,
outboard, inboard,
or best dressed boat

Heather Wastie

Below, from a 1971 newspaper clipping: *Accompanied by approving smiles from a boatman and his dog, Rally Queen Rosamund Bowen, aged 15 (centre) and her attendants Gillian Miller (left), also aged 15, Heather Thomas, aged 17, depart on a trip along the Staffordshire to Worcestershire canal after Alderman I. Harrington (behind them) had opened the rally.*

CATERING

Beefburgers and hot dogs

My husband, in his wisdom, decided that we would do the hot dogs and beefburgers for the rallies, over a weekend, Saturday and Sunday. We would cook over two thousand altogether. He always got the bread rolls and the buns from Robinson's in Netherton and the manageress got to know him. One day, he went to order them and there was a young lady behind the counter who ran out into the back and said, "*The man wants two thousand bread rolls!!*" The manageress came out and said, "*I knew it was you.*"

Ann Edwards

Grapefruit

We wanted to take the councillors through Coombs Wood [Gosty Hill] Tunnel to show them what it was like the other end and what the basin was like, entertaining them with a meal on the way. Two or three ladies helped me to produce a three-course meal. We were doing grapefruit for starter, a ham salad for the main meal and then I think it was fruit salad or something for the pudding. So quite simple really. But we hadn't got much room to prepare all this stuff. We had got all the grapefruit starters ready on the table - it was in the days when you cut a grapefruit in half, put a cherry on the top and sprinkled it with sugar - and we were going along with the councillors. We hit something under the water which tipped the boat sideways and all these grapefruits in their dishes slid off the table. I can remember we were all standing there with our arms out. The cooker tipped over as well.

But the councillors enjoyed it, and it did show them the state of the canal. In those days there was untold rubbish in the canal and it was a hazard all the time. It educated them, shall I say.

Sheila Smith

Catering for a work party

The main criterion was cheapness, the food was basic – full English breakfast, sandwiches and stew (hiding controversial ingredients like garlic and herbs and spices – lying about them when necessary!) and boiled fruit for afters, all cooked on ancient 4-ringed stoves (with one ring dead), by women with jobs, busy lives and no time to bake cakes in advance. Cakes and buns were bought. Claire and I paid upfront and got our money back at the camp.

We did have one disaster when Graham Palmer decided to get publicity during a work camp in Shropshire by inviting all the locals to bring someone. Bad move. They turned up with parents, siblings, girlfriends, girlfriends' parents, everybody's friends. Claire and I had been told to cater for "*about 30-35*". The queue wound round the village hall and out of the door – around 80 were eventually counted. We had been a bit wary and cooked mince and mash that could stretch to about 60. At the end, when people had stopped coming and Claire and I were looking at the small amount left, in strolled Graham and Mike Day and Megan demanding food and not pleased with what was on offer. We invited them to count the numbers who had turned up and to suggest where on a Saturday night more supplies could have come from. I could see that Graham understood the problem and he never tried that one again. A local came to our rescue by raiding her freezer for some bread and a packet of fish fingers, which is what Claire and I ate.

Graham paid a lot of attention to detail and really cared about the volunteers. The group who used to meet in someone's flat to collate the early Navvies magazine were always rewarded by cans of beer (boy, how we needed it too) and the sessions were always fun. During the working parties he would check that people were occupied and sort out any problems. After supper we would all head for the pub (which he had alerted beforehand) and he would do his best to keep us from waking the locals as we went home – not an easy task.   **Margaret Gibson**

CAMPAIGNING

Organising a cruise

I organised a cruise, all the way from the top end of the Staffs and Worcs Canal to the bottom end, and invited some members of the council to come and join us. That was a big undertaking because we fetched them, entertained them from A to B, took them back and then collected the next lot. We divided the canal up into sections and I had to work out where we were going to start each time and where we would have to stop ready for the next trip. I had to write to the councillors and organise people to pick them up, all Canal Society volunteers. So it took a lot of thought. It went all right; we didn't have any real mishaps and it impressed on all the councillors what an asset they'd got in their area which needed looking after. I won an award for that. It was presented to me at the Canal Society Dinner.

Sheila Smith

Sheila was awarded a prize for her work – a copy of Teddy Edwards' book, Inland Waterways of Great Britain, with these words printed inside and signed by the author:

This book is donated with great pleasure, and indeed pride, to Sheila Smith for the most meritorious deed relating to the work of the Staffordshire and Worcestershire Canal Society, during 1972. The occasion was the celebration of this great anniversary, the Bi-Centenary of the opening of the Canal, the only one Brindley saw to its completion. The celebration took the form of a cruise from Great Haywood Junction to Stourport, during the week May 21st to the 27th, when 27 members spent 316 hours, travelling 1513 miles to convey 59 guests. She organised this herself involving in the process every local authority through which the canal traverses. It is indeed fitting that the meticulous organisation of this event matched the meticulous work of Brindley himself.

Protest cruise on the Caldon Canal

We joined a protest cruise up the Caldon Canal. It was a rough canal and we had a small cruiser. We were going to be the first boat to go through Leek Tunnel since 1932. It would have been before 1969. It was November, a freezing cold morning, and of course it was me who had to scrape the ice off the front of the boat. The first lock we came to, before the tunnel, was covered in pieces of plywood or hardboard to block the holes [sluices to fill/empty the lock] and stop the water coming through. We had to strip all those off. All the ladies did that while the men were looking after the boats.

A little way into the tunnel there was no towpath – it had disappeared into the canal – so about fourteen people jumped onto our boat. We kept going, then came to a huge blockage. There was no way we were going to get through. It was about half past one and nobody had had anything to eat. They couldn't get back to their own boats because there was no towpath and we couldn't turn round. Everybody was hungry and I'd made a huge steak and kidney pudding, so I said, "*There isn't enough for fourteen people, but if we boil some potatoes we can manage.*" So I got everybody peeling potatoes and we made a meal. I thought about the wartime steamed pudding. I had flour and margarine etc on the boat, so I got the ladies working on it and we cooked it. I used to make my own jam, so we covered it in plum jam. Everybody enjoyed it. Eventually we could turn the boat round – it was only twenty foot – and took everybody back.

Jean Dobbs

Labouring at the Black Country Museum

There were a lot of sunken boats in the arm by the lime kilns and I remember helping to get them out and break them up. The children played in the mud and got mud all over them. One time, I think they were repairing one of the walls at the side of the canal, and I remember loading bricks into a little dinghy and ferrying them to where they were doing the work. I helped with the labour, and also provided drinks and food for everyone.

Rosemary Phillips

Waterways not Slaughterways
Words found in our interview with Rosemary Carden

I didn't do any physical work,
digging or stuff like that,
I took photos wherever I could.
You've got to publicise things!

My job involved a typewriter,
bombarding people on paper
or standing up at meetings
shouting from the back:

*Waterways not Slaughterways –
polluting, inefficient!
What you should be doing
is using our canals!*

A constant conveyor belt of boats
at four miles an hour
is better for the environment,
the cleanest, greenest way.

Heather Wastie

> I must say that I find the idea of the New City simply appalling, we have just returned from a journey through the area, the canal winds through some of the most beautiful and tranquil scenery in this part of Buckinghamshire. All those fields gently undulating on either side, to be covered with boxes and blocks of offices and Flats? Ugh. Enough.
>
> Yours,
>
> Rosemary Carden (Mrs.)

Snippet from a letter written by Rosemary Carden in 1970 about the rapidly expanding Milton Keynes.

Lorna Thomas
Words found in an article about Lorna by David Bolton, Waterways World, February 2001

Lorna's calm and charming manner
and underlying persuasiveness
overcame many obstacles

With husband Rhodes in Sapperton Tunnel
they hauled their small inflatable boat
over several roof falls,

scrambled over piles of rubble,
reached the final,
impassable blockage.

Tremendously hard, says Lorna,
the boat was heavy,
conditions tricky.

Recording their feat,
a Fasham-made plaque
hammered onto the wall.

Did she not find the darkness daunting?
Lorna smiles and calmly replies
We lived to tell the tale

Heather Wastie

They made this expedition with Bert Dunkley, Edwin and Andrew Fasham from the Coventry Canal Society in March 1959. The dinghy was affectionately known as Windbag. Lorna and Rhodes were involved in campaigns across the country, including at Stourbridge. They made several trips into Dudley Tunnel in Windbag.

Felice Pearson
Words found in an article by David Bolton, Waterways World, July 1993

Known to her friends as Felix,
this ardent and dedicated worker,
a cornerstone in the fight
to save our waterways,

was placed in the bow of a dinghy
known as the Blue Bath,
commanded to hold a torch
to show their hazardous path.

*'Speeding full tilt in the dark,
with this pitiful little light
expecting a barrier of bricks,
was a terrifying sight.*

*We thought we might sink in the tunnel
when no-one knew we were there!
Then we perceived a glimmer of light,
and breathed the pure fresh air...'*

Proving it wasn't blocked at all,
as British Waterways said,
they hadn't believed what they were told,
but saw for themselves instead.

Heather Wastie

Felix travelled through Dudley Tunnel with Robert Aickman and Crick Grundy. The date is not given in David's article.

TAKING ON AUTHORITY

Dredger in the way

There was three inches of ice and it was bitterly cold. We set off down the Erewash with the two boats, smashing as much ice as we could, rocking them like mad, using them as ice breakers, making a channel for the little boat. That was Soldanella – Susy and Max Ackermann. They just stayed behind and came down the open channel. (Susy and Max went on campaigning right till the day they died.)

We eventually got down to Stanton where the hot water came in from the iron works and all the ice had gone so we no longer had to rock. We tied up and left the boat till the following weekend when we had to get her back up to our mooring at Swarkestone because there was a stoppage due on Swarkestone Lock on the Monday morning. We got to Weston Cliff and there was a dredger with its legs down. There was no way we could get past and there was nobody around. They'd just left it. They had decided that nobody was going to be cruising in that sort of weather, and the stoppage was due to start, so they left the dredger where it was.

No mobile phones, nothing. Couldn't get hold of anyone on a Sunday afternoon. No car of course. We'd got to get back to our car. So there we were, stuck for the night. First thing in the morning the men arrived at the dredger. I said, "*Can't we get the stoppage held, just for a little while, so we can get through. After all, it's you that's stopped us.*" They said they'd do their best, but without any phones…

So we got to Swarkestone Lock and they'd stopped it. They put the planks in and drained it. So I went up the management tree till I got to someone who apologised. That was what probably started me off being militant.

Margaret Clark

A Canal Journey with my Mother
Words found in a tribute to Edith, known as Edie, by her son Graham

This may not be quite
What you are looking for
But anyway, here it is

Mum's no longer here
To tell her tale
The part she played
A small part in canal restoration

She didn't drive
Had no one
Who shared her interests
To drive her anywhere

Grew up on a farm
A life of limited possibilities
Then
Before the outbreak of war
Moved to a house
By the bank
Of the Walsall Canal

Lived in dread
We'd fall in
We never did

Loved the flow
The sounds
Of Life
Of Nature
Birdsong
A passing boat horse
That feeling
Of being able to breathe
Pure air again

Sunday mornings
Mum and I
Through Dudley Tunnel
And back

When I moved away
Mum still went
To every canal event
She could
Though never too involved
Maybe she felt
As a working class woman
No qualifications
She had too little to offer

My passion for waterways
Had its roots
In Mum's great enthusiasm
Our discussions over cuttings
From canal magazines
Collected specially for me

She never got her feet muddy
Nor her hands wet
Never wrote to a paper
Or lobbied a councillor
Always, though, fed my interest
Nurtured in me a passion
For the restoration of our canals

Encouraged her brother
To take his family
On canal holidays
Though never did herself

My mum
Beavering away
Quietly
In the background

All her tiny victories
Have left me with
Something I have now
To share
Not quite what you were looking for
But here it is

Rajan Naidu

October 1974 Stourbridge work party – from a slide transparency in Alan T Smith collection

Histrionic water

In Wolverhampton,
fish take me by surprise.

Looking down from Broad Street Bridge,
then from the towpath edge

I need an explanation
for such unexpected clarity,

a long exposure of minnows,
lush reeds and sulky sediment.

It's ironic, says the cut water,
I have been cleansed

by a vandal-induced stoppage.
Tearfully the water speaks:

It was you who saved me
from oil slick, effluent, blackened

polystyrene icebergs, mattress tangled
shopping trolleys, half inched bikes,

malicious metal spikes,
contents of living rooms tipped.

I was soap sud soup with beer bottle croutons,
peppered with cans and the odd chunk of meat.

You saved me from scum,
from smothering polythene,

wire running red, the callous garrottes
of those who would see me dead.

I fear the onset of duck weed.
You saved me to be stirred.

Heather Wastie

GLOSSARY

Bow hauling Pulling a boat – usually the butty – into a lock by hand by means of a rope

Butty Unpowered narrow boat

Cut Canal

Pound The stretch of water in between locks

Shear pin An easily replaceable pin inserted in an engine and designed to stop the machine by shearing if the load becomes too great

Silver Sword A scheme by the IWA to encourage boaters to tackle the most derelict parts of the waterway system, thereby helping to keep the channel open. To qualify for the award, boaters collected points by executing various tasks and keeping a log to prove it.

Swarf Debris

The Waterway Recovery Group (WRG), founded in 1970, is the national co-ordinating body for voluntary labour on the inland waterways of the United Kingdom

SOURCES

Aickman Archive is held by The National Archive at Kew

Navvies began as 'Navvies Notebook' in 1966 'Published by the Working Party Group of the London & Home Counties Branch, Inland Waterways Association'. In 1971 the title was shortened to 'Navvies'. All back copies are available on the Inland Waterways Association (IWA) Waterways Recovery Group website https://www.waterways.org.uk/wrg/

Waterways World is the biggest-selling and longest-established inland waterways magazine https://www.waterwaysworld.com/

ACKNOWLEDGEMENTS

p 34 ASHTAC photo by Harry Arnold MBE, reproduced by kind permission of Julie Arnold, Waterway Images Ltd

ABOUT US

Alarum Theatre specialise in telling the stories of ordinary women doing extraordinary things. In summer 2016 they began touring their first show, *Idle Women of the Wartime Waterways*, and in 2017 were awarded Arts Council funding for a 15-week 50 show tour which was Commended at the 2018 Canal & River Trust Living Waterways Awards. After seven tours across the country, the show is now available for one-off bookings, and a new double bill, *Acts of Abandon*, began touring in 2019.

Boater, writer, storyteller and actor Kate Saffin has lived on a narrowboat and told stories of the waterways as solo plays since 1999. She trained as a writer for stage and broadcast media at the Royal Central School of Speech and Drama (MFA). She adapted the waterway classic *Ramlin Rose: the Boatwoman's story* by Sheila Stewart and has performed at canal festivals, in pub gardens and at Edinburgh Festival Fringe. Other canal based plays have retold the apparently true story of a brothel on a boat (*The Mary Rose: A Boat of Ill Repute*), a late coming of age for a pensioner who finds herself on holiday on a boat (*Finding Libby*) and a musical based on *Midsummer Milly*, a story for children from the Muddy Waters series by Dan Clacher.

Poet, singer-songwriter and accordion player Heather Wastie has been involved with canals since childhood, when her family took part in campaigns to save them. Her writing projects include a Residency at the Museum of Carpet, culminating in a book *Weaving Yarns*, published by Black Pear Press. She was the 2015/16 Worcestershire Poet Laureate and in 2017 was commissioned to write and perform poems for the popular Nationwide Building Society television ad campaign. In 2018 she completed a book of poems about the restoration of the Droitwich Canals, *The Muck and Shovel Brigade*, commissioned by Canal & River Trust for The Ring. This work is now touring as half of Alarum's double bill, *Acts of Abandon*, along with Kate's play *The Mary Rose: A Boat of Ill Repute*.

This project would not have been possible without the support of the National Lottery Heritage Fund.

Thanks also to:

ABNB Boat Brokerage
Barlow Theatre, Oldbury
BCN Society
Canal & River Trust Archive, Ellesmere Port
Carolyn Clark
Dudley Canal and Tunnel Trust
Erin Hopkins – Film Maker
Geoff Broadway – Living Memory Project
Hilary & Mike Skidmore – DCTT Archive volunteers
Jenni Waugh – External evaluator
Dr Jodie Matthews
Julia Letts – Oral History Trainer
Laura Ndjoli and University of Worcester Design Dept
Nicola Bolton
Staffordshire & Worcestershire Canal Society
Stourbridge Navigation Trust
Tipton Canal Festival
Tipton Civic Society – Keith Hodgkins
Tipton Library - Robert Hazel

Interviewees: (see back cover photo from top L): Rosemary Phillips, Hazel Platzer, Rosemary Carden, Sammy Rose, Heather Wastie, Sheila Smith, Jose Wyles, Maureen Griffiths, Jane Henderson, Ann Edwards, Tina Gittings, Beryl McDowall, Jeni Hatton, Gillian Whittaker, Caroline Whittaker, Jean Dobbs, Mavis Waldron, Penny Clover, Margaret Clark

Volunteers: Carolyn Theobold, Fabian Hiscock, Helen Underhill, Jane Lowthion, Julia Fallon, Kerstin Exner, Kit Acott, Lesley Jordan, Lois Parker, Maarja Kaaristo, Mark Robinson, Sarah Jackson, Su Vale, Liz Wigglesworth

Everyone who spoke to us, recorded interviews or wrote on our story wall at one of our many events; anyone who sent contributions by email; anyone who put money in our donations jar... It is impossible to thank you all.